WE
ARE ALL
CONNECTED

CARING FOR EACH OTHER & THE EARTH

by Gabi Garcia

illustrated by
Natalia Jimenez Osorio

We all live on one blue dot spinning in space.
We are all a part of one human race.

We have hopes and dreams and love in our hearts.
We are stronger together than we are apart.

So why all the fuss to compete and compare,

when it feels so much better to connect and to share.

We can share when we're sad, or down in the dumps.

We can share our joys, give high fives or fist bumps.

When we're seen and heard, trust blooms and grows.
WE ARE ALL CONNECTED. Kindness ripples and flows.

Let's speak up for others, include and embrace.
We all make mistakes. We can give others grace.

We have more in common than we may believe.
WE ARE ALL CONNECTED. We all love, we all grieve.

We can celebrate differences, lend a hand.
Learn from each other, take a stand.

WE ARE ALL CONNECTED. Let's raise our voices.

We can work together to make brave choices.

Protect the water, care for the land,
Respect all beings; the earth is grand.

Nature gives her bounty. She is gentle yet mighty.
Stand in awe of her force, preserve her beauty.

Let's look under rocks and explore vast skies, honor the mountains and chase butterflies.

Let's go hunting for rainbows, plant more trees,

grow a garden and be friends with bees.

The earth is our home and needs our care.

We all play a part. We breathe the same air.

we belong to the earth-- it is not ours.
WE ARE ALL CONNECTED. We are made of stars.

TAKE CARE OF EACH OTHER.

TAKE CARE OF THE EARTH.
WE ARE ALL HERE TOGETHER.

FOR LILIANA

902 Gardner Road no. 4
Austin, Texas 78721
skinned knee
publishing

Publisher's Cataloging-in-Publication data
Names: Garcia, Gabi, author. | Jimenez Osorio, Natalia, illustrator.
Title: We are all connected : caring for each other & the earth / written by Gabi Garcia; illustrated by Natalia Jimenez Osorio.
Description: Austin, TX: Skinned Knee Publishing, 2022. | Summary: A poem that celebrates the interconnectedness of the world and reminds humans to come together to protect the Earth and care for each other.
Identifiers: ISBN: 978-1-949633-51-1 (hardcover) | 978-1-949633-37-5 (paperback) | 978-1-949633-53-5 (ebook)
Subjects: LCSH Friendship--Juvenile literature. | Social justice--Juvenile literature. | Environmental protection--Citizen participation--Juvenile literature. | Conservation of natural resources--Juvenile literature. | Nature--Effect of human beings on--Juvenile literature. | Human ecology--Juvenile literature. | BISAC JUVENILE NONFICTION / Social Topics / Friendship | JUVENILE NONFICTION / Recycling & Green Living | JUVENILE NONFICTION / Science & Nature / Environmental Conservation & Protection
Classification: LCC TD171. .G33 2022| DDC 333.7/2--dc23

Thank you for choosing this book!

I believe in the power and beauty of books. I hope that the ones I write will contribute in some small way toward making this world a better place.

Visit gabigarciabooks.com for downloadable activities that accompany this book.

ALL TITLES AVAILABLE IN SPANISH

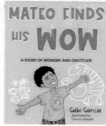

Natalia Jiménez Osorio is a Colombian illustrator & animator based in The Netherlands. She is represented by Astound Agency.

Made in the USA
Las Vegas, NV
30 March 2024

87995209R00021